Strength Beyond Limits

Building Resilience and Confidence

By
Liam Seaton

Strength Beyond Limits: Building Resilience and Confidence

Author: Liam Seaton

Copyright © 2025 Liam Seaton

The right of Liam Seaton to be identified as author of this work has been asserted by the author in accordance with section 77 and 78 of the Copyright, Designs and Patents Act 1988.

ISBN 978-1-83538-582-1 (Paperback)
978-1-83538-583-8 (E-Book)

Cover Design and Book Layout by:
Maple Publishers
www.maplepublishers.com

Published by:
Maple Publishers
Fairbourne Drive, Atterbury,
Milton Keynes,
MK10 9RG, UK
www.maplepublishers.com

A CIP catalogue record for this title is available from the British Library.

All rights reserved. No part of this book may be reproduced or translated by any form or by any means, electronic or mechanical, including photocopying, recording or by any information storage and retrieval system without written permission from the author.

The views expressed in this work are solely those of the author and do not reflect the opinions of Publishers, and the Publisher hereby disclaims any responsibility for them. This book should not be used as a substitute for the advice of a competent authority, admitted or authorized to advise on the subjects covered.

Contents

Introduction 4

Chapter 1 – A New Beginning 6

Chapter 2 – Finding Your Strength 9

Chapter 3 – Taking Control of Your Journey 15

Chapter 4 – Embracing the Challenges Ahead 21

Chapter 5 – Rolling Into the Gym: A New Kind of Strength 24

Chapter 6 – Building Your Routine 27

Chapter 7 – Nutrition and Recovery 29

Chapter 8 – Overcoming Mental Hurdles 32

Chapter 9 – Empowering Yourself and Others 34

Chapter 10 – The Next Step 36

Chapter 11 – Thriving Beyond the Gym 38

Chapter 12 – Your Legacy of Strength 42

Introduction

Hey, I'm Liam, and this book is my story — a story that I hope resonates with you and reminds you that no matter where you are right now, you can rise, adapt, and rediscover your strength.

This isn't just about fitness; it's about finding strength in every form — physical, mental, emotional, and spiritual. I'm not an expert or a professional trainer, but I've walked a path that's taught me more about strength than I could have ever imagined. I've faced life-altering changes, I've had moments of doubt, and I've felt the weight of challenges that seemed impossible to overcome. But I've also learned how to rise from those moments, how to adapt when life pushes me down, and how to rebuild my strength — in all aspects of my life.

This book is for anyone who's starting fresh. Whether you're adjusting to life in a wheelchair, navigating the world as an amputee, or simply looking to become a stronger, healthier version of yourself, this journey is for you. It's a guide, a companion, and a reminder that you're not alone in this.

We'll talk about everything — from the mindset it takes to push through the tough days to rolling into the gym for the first time and embracing those challenges as opportunities. I'll share personal stories, practical advice, and insights I've picked up along the way in the hope that they help you too.

I'll be honest: you won't find perfection here. I don't have all the answers. I'm still learning, just like you. But what I've discovered is this — when we stop focusing on what we can't do, The first step is always the hardest. Whether you're just learning to roll forward in a wheelchair, taking your first steps with a prosthetic, or simply adjusting to a life that feels different, it's okay to feel unsure. But remember, you're not starting from scratch; you're starting from experience.

The world may have shifted beneath your feet, but this isn't the end of your journey. It's the beginning of something new — a new chapter filled with growth, strength, and resilience. You may not see it right now, but inside of you is an incredible power, a drive to keep pushing, to keep moving forward, no matter the obstacles.

There's no "one way" to go about this. The path to strength, confidence, and self-love will look different for each person. But one thing is certain — you *can* get there. Every small victory, every moment of progress, is a testament to the incredible resilience you've always had, even when you didn't realize it.

In this book, we'll talk about how to embrace your journey, take control of your health, build strength, and love yourself fully — exactly as you are. Whether you're here to conquer the gym, find a new passion, or just take that first step into a new day, this is your space to grow, adapt, and thrive.

It's time to turn the page and step into the life you deserve and instead start believing in what we *can* do, that's when we unlock our true strength.

This journey isn't just about lifting weights or reaching fitness goals. It's about lifting yourself up, discovering what you're truly capable of, and using that strength to build a life that's empowering and fulfilling.

So, whether this is your first step or your hundredth, know that this is only the beginning. Your story is still being written. Let's take that next step together, because I believe your journey is about to get even stronger.

Chapter 1
A New Beginning

Finding Your Strength

When you're faced with a major life change, like becoming an amputee or using a wheelchair for the first time, it's easy to feel overwhelmed by everything that's ahead. The unknowns can feel daunting, and fear can creep in. But what if I told you that this new chapter holds the potential for strength you never thought possible?

Strength is not just physical. It's mental, emotional, and spiritual. You are stronger than you think, and you have a well of resilience within you that's just waiting to be tapped into. Whether it's the strength to lift a weight in the gym, the courage to try something new, or the determination to face a tough day, you'll find that your capacity to endure, adapt, and thrive grows with every challenge you face.

But first, you need to believe in that strength. This book isn't just about working out or learning to live with your disability; it's about reclaiming your power. It's about realizing that just because your circumstances have changed doesn't mean who you are or what you're capable of has to change. You can redefine yourself, your body, your abilities — all of it. And the first step in doing that is recognizing that you already have everything you need to succeed.

You might not see it yet, but you're capable of achieving things you've never imagined. The strength you'll discover in yourself won't be limited by your new reality — it will be fueled by it. You've already overcome more than you know, and the best part is, the journey is just getting started.

Taking Control of Your Journey

For many of us, becoming an amputee or learning to live with a disability is unexpected. The moment it happens can feel like everything is out of your control. But the truth is, while you may not be able to control what happened to you, you can control how you respond. You can control how you move forward.

The journey ahead will have its ups and downs, but what matters most is that you keep moving. Every day is an opportunity to make a choice: to fight for your well-being, to build your strength, and to grow into the person you want to be. It's okay if it feels slow at first. Change doesn't happen overnight, but small, consistent steps will lead to big results. Every bit of progress counts, and no matter how small the victories seem, they are the foundation of your transformation.

This book will give you the tools and the mindset to take control of your fitness, health, and life in a way that suits your body and your unique journey. We'll explore everything from setting realistic fitness goals, adapting exercises, and building a routine to fueling your body with the right nutrition. You'll also learn how to overcome the mental hurdles that come with change — how to shift your mindset from "I can't" to "I can."

Remember, the only limit to your potential is the one you place on yourself. You are capable of more than you think. Let's start this journey together — one step at a time.

Embracing the Challenges Ahead

Challenges are part of life, but they don't define us. What defines us is how we respond when faced with those challenges. As someone who has experienced loss, change, or adversity, you already know that life isn't always easy. But with every challenge, there's an opportunity to grow stronger. Every moment you push through — no matter how tough it gets — adds to your power.

At times, you might want to give up. You might feel like the journey is too hard, or that you've hit a wall you can't climb. In those moments, remember this: you have an entire community of people who understand what you're going through, and you have the inner strength to break through those walls, brick by brick.

You will face days where everything seems impossible, but those are the days that matter most. Because on the other side of the struggle is your greatest strength, your deepest resilience. You'll surprise yourself. There's so much more in you than you realize.

The road ahead won't always be smooth, but with the right mindset, support, and drive, it will be a journey worth every step.

Chapter 2
Finding Your Strength

Physical Strength is Just the Start

When we think of strength, the first thing that often comes to mind is physical power: lifting weights, running long distances, or pushing our limits in the gym. And while physical strength is important, it's just one part of a much larger picture.

Physical strength is built by training the body — through lifting weights, building endurance, improving mobility, and mastering your body's movements. But what happens when physical strength isn't enough to get us through the hardest times? The truth is, physical strength is the foundation, but it's mental, emotional, and spiritual strength that truly empowers us to keep going, even when our physical body is telling us to stop.

Strength is often viewed as something you either have or don't have — but that's a misconception. The reality is that strength comes in many forms. It's about perseverance, adaptability, and the will to rise up when life knocks you down. It's not about being the strongest in the room but about being your strongest version of yourself, no matter where you are starting from.

Physical strength builds the body, but it also builds mental resilience. It teaches us discipline and the power of small victories. But if we don't nurture the other aspects of our strength — our mind, emotions, and spirit — we're missing the full picture. This chapter will explore all the different dimensions of strength that will help you rise above challenges, big and small.

The Difference Between Physical, Mental, Emotional, and Spiritual Strength

To truly find your strength, you need to understand that strength isn't just measured by the weight you can lift or the distance you can travel. Strength is multidimensional. Let's break it down:

- **Physical Strength**: This is the most obvious form of strength. It's the strength you can see and feel when you push your body to its limits, whether it's through lifting, cardio, or stretching. But it's not just about building muscle — it's about mobility, flexibility, and stamina. It's about learning what your body can do, even when your circumstances change.

- **Mental Strength**: Mental strength is the ability to persevere through tough times, think critically, and overcome self-doubt. It's the voice inside your head that tells you, "I can do this," even when everything else is telling you otherwise. It's not about pushing through without feeling fear or anxiety, but about acknowledging those feelings and continuing anyway. Mental strength is about learning to silence negative thoughts and replacing them with affirmations of possibility.

- **Emotional Strength**: Emotional strength is the resilience to handle the ups and downs of life. It's about embracing vulnerability, feeling your emotions, and allowing yourself to heal. Emotions are not weaknesses — they are signals that guide us, helping us understand what we need. Emotional strength is found in learning how to process those emotions rather than letting them control you. It's about bouncing back after a setback and finding peace in your own feelings.

- **Spiritual Strength**: Spiritual strength isn't necessarily about religion (though it can be) — it's about finding meaning, purpose, and connection beyond yourself. It's having faith in your ability to overcome challenges and knowing that you have something greater within you. It's about developing inner peace, aligning with your values, and drawing strength from your beliefs. Whether you find spirituality in nature, meditation, or a higher power, spiritual strength connects you to your purpose and provides an unwavering source of support.

Each of these areas of strength is connected. When you work on one, the others improve. Physical training builds mental toughness. Emotional self-care leads to a clearer mind. Spiritual practices ground you and offer clarity when things feel uncertain. Finding balance in all of these areas is key to becoming truly strong.

Why Strength Comes in Many Forms

You may have heard people say, "Strength isn't just physical." It sounds like a cliché, but it's absolutely true. Strength comes in many forms, and each form serves a different purpose. The best part is that all of these strengths are within you, ready to be cultivated.

Strength isn't something that only exists in a gym. It exists in your ability to face hardship and keep moving forward. It shows up in your daily decisions, in how you respond to challenges, and in your ability to adapt. When you face a setback or an obstacle, strength is what helps you keep going. It's the ability to pivot, adapt, and keep working toward your goals, no matter the circumstances.

In the gym, you will build physical strength. But in life, you build mental, emotional, and spiritual strength every day. And these strengths will guide you, not just in fitness, but in every area of your life. They will help you break through barriers, find new opportunities, and rise after each fall.

Remember, strength doesn't always look the way society expects it to. It's not about having the most muscle or running the fastest time. Sometimes, strength is about showing up when you don't feel like it. It's about being kind to yourself when you struggle. It's about learning, growing, and getting back up when life knocks you down. That's true strength.

Reclaiming Your Power

In the wake of significant change — whether it's due to an accident, an injury, or another life-altering event — it's easy to feel like you've lost control. You may feel powerless, as though the world has shifted beneath your feet. It's natural to grieve the loss of what you once knew. But I want to remind you that your power has not been taken away from you. It's still there, waiting to be reclaimed.

Reclaiming your power is about taking back control of your life, your choices, and your path. It's about shifting your mindset from "I can't" to "I can" and embracing the new possibilities ahead of you. You've faced something difficult, but now it's time to turn that challenge into your greatest strength.

- **Start with Small Wins**: Reclaiming your power doesn't mean you need to change everything overnight. It's about finding small victories each day. Maybe today, it's rolling yourself into the gym. Tomorrow, it's completing a full workout or hitting a new personal best. These small wins build momentum, and momentum builds confidence. **Shift Your Mindset**: Power comes from within. Change your inner narrative from "I'm broken" to "I am resilient." The words you tell yourself shape how you see the world and yourself. Choose an empowering language. Remind yourself that you are still you — capable, worthy, and strong.

- **Surround Yourself with Support**: Reclaiming your power doesn't mean doing it alone. Surround yourself with people who believe in you, who uplift and encourage you. Whether it's family, friends, or a community of like-minded individuals, connection strengthens your resolve.

How to Rebuild Self-Esteem and Confidence After Change

When life changes unexpectedly, it can feel like a direct hit to your self-esteem and confidence. You may wonder who you are now, without the abilities or life you once had. But here's the truth: You are still you.

You are still strong. You are still worthy. And it's entirely possible to rebuild your self-esteem and confidence from the ground up.

- **Start by Acknowledging Your Strengths**: Take inventory of your strengths, both past and present. Write down everything you've overcome so far — every challenge, every moment of resilience. Remind yourself of who you've been and who you still are. These accomplishments, big or small, are proof of your strength.
- **Practice Self-Compassion**: Be kind to yourself. You don't need to be perfect, and you don't need to have everything figured out right away. It's okay to have bad days, to struggle, and to feel frustrated. Treat yourself with the same kindness and understanding that you would offer a friend going through a tough time.
- **Set Realistic Goals and Celebrate Progress**: Self-esteem comes from achievement, but achievement doesn't always mean perfection. Set small, realistic goals and celebrate each milestone along the way. Whether it's getting through a tough workout, trying a new exercise, or simply showing up, every step forward is worth celebrating.
- **Build a Supportive Environment**: Confidence thrives in a positive, supportive environment. Surround yourself with people who lift you up and celebrate your progress. Distance yourself from negativity or anyone who doesn't see your potential.

Setting the Foundation for a Journey of Personal Empowerment

Reclaiming your strength and rebuilding your confidence isn't an overnight process. But every small step you take toward personal empowerment will create a solid foundation for lasting change. This journey is ongoing. The strength you cultivate today will be the strength you rely on tomorrow.

Remember: Empowerment comes from within. It's about embracing who you are — imperfections and all — and deciding that you are enough. It's about setting your own path, finding your purpose, and moving forward with confidence, no matter the obstacles in your way.

This journey isn't just about physical strength. It's about mental, emotional, and spiritual growth. It's about becoming the best version of yourself — someone who is resilient, empowered, and unstoppable.

Chapter 3
Taking Control of Your Journey

Own Your Story

One of the most powerful things you can do on this journey is **own your story**. The past, the struggles, the triumphs, and the lessons — they all make you who you are today. No matter what has happened in your life, no matter the challenges you've faced, your story is yours to tell. It's not just about what you've been through, but about how you've responded to it, how you've grown from it, and how you've used it to shape your future.

Owning your story is the first step in taking control of your journey. It means acknowledging the truth of your experiences — both the good and the bad — and deciding to move forward on your own terms. It's about no longer being defined by the things you can't change but instead defining yourself by the way you choose to rise above them.

When you own your story, you take back the narrative. You no longer let fear, doubt, or circumstances dictate your actions. You become the author of your life, and this gives you the power to create the future you want.

Why is this important? Because when you own your story, you realize that you have always had the power to shape your life. You may not have chosen every challenge you've faced, but you can choose how you respond. You can choose to find strength in your experiences, to learn from them, and to create a new narrative — one of resilience, hope, and empowerment.

Shifting from "I Can't" to "I Can"

The most common barrier we face when starting a new journey is self-doubt. You may find yourself thinking, "I can't do this," "I'm not strong enough," or "This isn't for me." These thoughts are natural when you're stepping into the unknown. However, if you let these thoughts dictate your actions, they will keep you stuck.

The key to overcoming these barriers is **shifting your mindset from "I can't" to "I can."** It's about reprogramming the way you talk to yourself and replacing limiting beliefs with empowering affirmations. Instead of thinking, "I can't lift this weight," ask yourself, "What can I do today to get stronger?" Instead of, "I'm not strong enough to be in the gym," ask yourself, "What's one small action I can take today to improve?"

This shift doesn't happen overnight, but it's one of the most powerful things you can do for your personal growth. **Mindset is everything.** The way you see yourself determines the way you show up in the world. So, if you begin to believe in your own strength, it's incredible what you can accomplish.

One way to shift this mindset is through **positive self-talk**. Start every day with affirmations — even if they feel unnatural at first. Say things like:

- "I am capable."
- "I am stronger than I think."
- "I will improve every day, no matter how small the progress."
- "I can overcome any obstacle."

It may sound simple, but consistent positive self-talk will slowly replace your negative thought patterns and empower you to take control of your actions.

Overcoming Setbacks and Pushing Past Fear

Setbacks are inevitable — no one's journey is perfectly linear. You will have days where things don't go as planned, where progress feels slow, or where you feel like giving up. But setbacks aren't failures. **They're part of the process.**

When you experience a setback, it's important not to see it as a roadblock but as an opportunity for growth. Every setback holds a lesson. Perhaps it's a sign that you need to adjust your approach. Maybe it's a reminder to take a break and rest. Or it could be an opportunity to dig deeper into your motivation and commitment.

The key is how you respond to setbacks. When they come, instead of getting discouraged or giving up, remind yourself that **every successful person has faced setbacks**. What makes them successful isn't avoiding failure but learning how to bounce back from it.

Pushing past fear is a crucial part of overcoming setbacks. Fear will always be there, whether it's fear of failure, fear of judgment, or fear of the unknown. But fear doesn't have to control you. One effective strategy is to approach fear with curiosity. Ask yourself, "What is this fear trying to teach me?"

The more you face fear head-on, the more you build your mental and emotional resilience. Take small steps outside your comfort zone, and each time you do, you'll find that the fear loses its grip. With time, you'll begin to realize that **the biggest obstacles are often the ones we've built in our own minds.**

Strength in Patience - one of many setbacks.

Mum and I wheeled into the clinic with cautious optimism. Today was supposed to be the day we got answers. After everything I'd been through, I was hoping for good news, though part of me was still bracing for disappointment.

This wasn't even the first time I'd tried to make it here. Three weeks earlier, I'd missed my appointment because patient transport canceled on me—an hour after they were supposed to pick me up. That delay meant another week of waiting for a new X-ray, and now, even more time before I could hear how my ankle was healing. It was frustrating, but I told myself to push through.

The nurse led me into the X-ray room, and the process was over quickly. Afterward, Mum and I headed back out to the waiting area. The minutes dragged on, and I kept glancing at the door, willing the doctor to call me in with some good news.

"Do you think this'll be the one?" I asked Mum quietly. "Do you think I'll finally be able to start standing?"

She smiled gently. "Whatever happens, Liam, you're moving forward. It's all part of the process."

Finally, we were called back in. The doctor was holding the fresh X-rays, her face serious as she pulled up the images on the screen. I leaned forward, eager to hear what she had to say.

"Well," she began, "your ankle is healing... but not as fast as I'd hoped. I'd like to give it two more weeks before we start weight-bearing. Just to be sure."

I felt my heart sink. Two more weeks. That made it six weeks total since I'd first been supposed to get this news. All the excitement I'd felt earlier disappeared, replaced by a wave of frustration and helplessness. Mum must've noticed because she put her hand on my shoulder as we left the room.

The drive home was quiet at first. I stared out the window, trying to make sense of my emotions. "Why does this keep happening?" I finally muttered. "First the canceled appointment, now this. It's like I'll never get there."

Mum glanced at me. "I know it's hard," she said, "but you're still moving forward, even if it's slower than you'd like. These two weeks are just another chance to get stronger, to prepare."

Her words stuck with me. When we got home, I went straight to my computer and started typing. I wrote about the canceled appointment, the delays, the setbacks. Getting it all out felt cathartic. But as I wrote, something clicked. This wasn't a sign to give up—it was an opportunity to start.

I decided to focus on what I *could* do during the next two weeks. I researched exercises I could do in my chair to start building strength and flexibility. I set goals to improve my nutrition and mental health. By the time I finished typing, I had a plan—and for the first time that day, I felt hopeful again.

Sure, the wait was longer than I'd wanted, but it wasn't wasted. Those two weeks became the foundation for everything I was about to achieve. When the time finally came to stand, I wouldn't just be ready—I'd be stronger for having waited.

Goal Setting and Progress

One of the most empowering tools in your journey is the ability to set goals. **Goal setting** gives you direction and purpose. It helps you break down your big dreams into actionable steps and keeps you motivated even when things get tough.

However, goal setting isn't just about dreaming big; it's about setting **realistic, achievable goals** that you can actually work toward. You're not going to transform overnight, and that's okay. Setting goals gives you a roadmap for progress.

Here's how to break down effective goals for your journey:

1. **Set Clear, Specific Goals**:

   Instead of saying, "I want to get stronger," say, "I will be able to lift 5 more pounds on my bench press in 6 weeks." The more specific your goals are, the easier it will be to track your progress.

2. **Make Goals Measurable**:

   How will you know you've succeeded? Make sure your goals have measurable outcomes, so you can track your progress over time. For example, if your goal is to increase your mobility, track the number of steps or the distance you can walk or roll each week.

3. **Break Goals Into Smaller, Actionable Steps**:

   Big goals can be overwhelming, so break them down into smaller, more manageable tasks. For example, if your goal is to work out three times a week, start by scheduling one day. Once you've mastered that, add another.

4. **Stay Realistic and Patient**:

    It's easy to set big, lofty goals — and that's great! But be realistic about the time, effort, and consistency required to reach them. Set your goals in a way that challenges you, but isn't so far out of reach that they feel impossible.

5. **Review and Adjust**:

    Your goals might change along the way, and that's okay. Life is unpredictable, and as you grow, your goals will evolve. Be flexible and adjust your goals as needed, but always keep your end vision in mind.

Celebrating Small Victories and Understanding That Progress is Personal

One of the most important aspects of goal setting is **celebrating small victories** along the way. It's easy to get caught up in the end goal and forget that every step forward — no matter how small — is a victory. Each rep, each extra set, each new skill learned, or even each day you show up is worth celebrating.

Why? Because **progress is personal**. It doesn't matter how fast someone else is moving or what their journey looks like. What matters is that you're making progress on your own path. Celebrate that!

Small victories create momentum and keep you motivated. They build your confidence and help you see that the work you're putting in is paying off. Even if the goal is still far off, every step forward is a reason to be proud.

For example, if your goal is to lift a certain weight, but today you only increased by a small amount, that's still progress. Or maybe you didn't reach your full goal this week, but you made it to the gym consistently — that is progress! Every time you push yourself, you grow stronger, even if it doesn't always feel like it.

Remember, **progress is a journey, not a destination**. It's about growth, not perfection. It's about showing up, learning, adapting, and improving.

Chapter 4
Embracing the Challenges Ahead

Turning Obstacles into Opportunities

Life is full of challenges, and while it's easy to see them as barriers, the truth is that obstacles can be turned into **opportunities for growth**. Challenges force us to think differently, adapt, and innovate. Instead of asking, "Why me?" when faced with adversity, ask, "What can I learn from this?" This shift in perspective is crucial to embracing the journey ahead.

For example, if you encounter an obstacle that limits your mobility or flexibility, instead of seeing it as something that holds you back, think of it as an opportunity to get creative. You might find new exercises or modify existing ones in ways that others haven't considered. **Obstacles push us to explore new solutions, expand our creativity, and discover strengths we didn't know we had.**

It's important to remember that your challenges are not roadblocks — they're stepping stones that can lead you to unexpected opportunities. They teach you patience, resilience, and the power of adaptability. The more you approach challenges with an open mind, the more you'll see them as opportunities to learn, grow, and ultimately thrive.

Reframing Challenges as Stepping Stones

A key element of embracing challenges is **reframing** them. When you encounter a setback, instead of thinking of it as a dead end, think of it as a learning experience. **Stepping stones** are not about perfection

— they're about progress. Each challenge you face is a chance to move forward, learn more about yourself, and improve in new ways.

Let's say you're learning a new exercise or movement and you hit a plateau. Instead of getting frustrated, view the plateau as a natural part of the process. **Stepping stones are built on effort, not perfection.** They're the incremental progress you make, even when it feels like you're not moving fast enough. Every time you encounter a challenge, you're building a stronger foundation for the next step.

Embracing Failure as Part of the Process

Failure is often seen as something to avoid, but it is actually a **necessary part of success.** It's in the moments where you fail that you learn your greatest lessons. Failure doesn't mean you've lost or that you're not capable. It means that you've tried something new, you've pushed your limits, and you've learned something that will help you improve.

Think about a time when you failed at something. What did you learn from it? Chances are, that failure gave you insights into how to approach the situation differently next time. **Failure is feedback.** It tells you what works and what doesn't. Embracing failure as part of the process means that you don't see it as a stopping point but as a springboard to the next attempt, the next opportunity, and the next success.

The Power of Persistence

Why is **persistence** so important? Because persistence is what keeps you going when things get tough. It's the driving force behind every success story. Persistence is the ability to push forward, even when progress feels slow or setbacks seem overwhelming. It's understanding that growth doesn't happen overnight — it's built one step at a time.

Persistence is often the difference between those who succeed and those who give up. It's the small actions you take every day — showing up, doing the work, and continuing to believe in yourself — that eventually lead to big changes. Whether you're facing a challenging workout, adapting to a new way of life, or overcoming self-doubt, persistence is your ally. **It's the foundation of resilience** and the key to long-term success.

Stories of Resilience and Overcoming Difficult Moments

Think about the most inspiring people in your life. Many of them likely faced incredible obstacles but overcame them with sheer resilience. Whether it's someone in your own life who has battled an injury or a well-known figure who faced adversity and succeeded, their stories are filled with perseverance.

For example, consider the story of athletes with disabilities who excel in adaptive sports. Despite facing major challenges, they've built successful careers by refusing not to give up. Their journeys are filled with setbacks, but their persistence kept them moving forward. **Persistence doesn't mean never failing; it means failing and getting up again.** It means using the lessons learned from failure to propel you toward success.

These stories of resilience remind us that no matter how difficult the road may seem, **we all have the strength to overcome our hardest moments**. It's not about avoiding hardship; it's about having the courage to face it head-on and keep pushing forward.

Chapter 5
Rolling Into the Gym: A New Kind of Strength

Your New Space: The Gym

The gym can feel intimidating, especially if it's a place where you haven't felt comfortable before. However, the gym is not just for able-bodied individuals or athletes. It is for everyone — **including you**. The gym is a space where you can grow stronger, both physically and mentally, in a supportive and empowering environment. **It's your space for self-improvement.**

As a wheelchair user or amputee, you may face unique challenges when navigating the gym, but that doesn't mean it's not for you. The key is to **adjust your mindset**. Rather than seeing the gym as a place where you don't belong, see it as an opportunity to **empower yourself**, push your limits, and become the strongest version of yourself. The gym is where you can redefine strength — not just in terms of how much weight you can lift, but in terms of how much courage and resilience you bring to your workouts.

The most important thing when stepping into the gym is **adjusting your expectations**. Start by understanding that **your fitness journey is your own**. It's not about comparing yourself to others, but about focusing on your personal goals, growth, and improvement.

Adjusting Your Mindset and Expectations for Gym Workouts

The gym can be a place where expectations are often skewed by what we see on social media or in magazines. But those ideals don't reflect your personal journey. **Your strength is not defined by the**

weights you lift or the time you spend on a treadmill. Your strength is defined by the effort you put in, the consistency you maintain, and the progress you make along the way.

It's okay if your workouts look different from someone else's. You're not there to compete with anyone but yourself. As a wheelchair user or amputee, you may need to modify exercises, but that doesn't diminish their value. **Every rep, every set, every moment of effort is a victory.**

Embracing the Gym as a Space for Empowerment, Not Comparison

It's easy to compare yourself to others, especially in a gym where people often seem to be further along in their fitness journey. However, this comparison can lead to self-doubt and discouragement. Instead, **embrace the gym as a space for empowerment**. It's your personal space to build strength, confidence, and resilience.

Remember, no two journeys are the same. Just because someone else is lifting more weight doesn't mean you aren't making progress. **Celebrate your own victories** and focus on your own growth. Every time you show up, you're taking steps toward your goals — and that is powerful.

Adapting Exercises for Your Body

In the gym, it's essential to modify exercises to meet your body's unique needs. For example, if you're in a wheelchair, some traditional exercises might need modification. You can still work your upper body, core, and other muscles — you just might need to find alternatives that work for you. **Adaptive fitness is about finding what works for your body** and modifying exercises accordingly. The key is to focus on movements that feel good and challenge your muscles.

When using accessible equipment, work with a trainer or coach who understands your needs. Many gyms offer adaptive fitness programs, or you can ask for advice on how to modify certain exercises to ensure they suit your abilities and goals.

Tips for Getting Started with Accessible Equipment

Start simple. Many gyms have machines and equipment that can be adapted for your needs. **Try starting with machines that provide support** for your body and allow you to focus on specific muscle groups. **Free weights and resistance bands** are also great tools for building strength and improving mobility.

Ask for assistance. If you're not sure how to use a piece of equipment, ask a trainer for help. Many trainers are knowledgeable about adaptive fitness and will be happy to assist you in finding the right approach.

The Mental Shift

The gym is not just about physical strength. It's also about **mental strength**. The mental shift that happens when you step into the gym is just as important as the physical strength you're building. **Building mental resilience** through exercise can help you push through challenges both inside and outside the gym.

When you feel discouraged, remember why you started. **Keep reminding yourself that every effort counts**. Each time you show up and give your best, you're building not just muscle but mental toughness.

Chapter 6
Building Your Routine

Creating a Sustainable Workout Plan

One of the most important things you can do for your fitness journey is to create a **sustainable workout plan**. It's easy to get excited and push yourself too hard at first, but the key is to build a plan that fits your current level and allows for gradual progress.

Start by setting **short-term and long-term goals** for your fitness. Short-term goals can help you stay motivated and track progress, while long-term goals can keep you focused on the bigger picture. **Make your plan flexible** so that if life gets in the way, you can adjust it instead of giving up completely.

The Importance of Consistency and Gradual Improvement

Consistency is key to long-term progress. **Small steps add up** over time, so rather than focusing on drastic change, focus on steady, sustainable improvement. Every workout, every effort you put in will compound over time.

Gradual improvement is the foundation of building both strength and endurance. The key is to take things one step at a time, so you don't overwhelm yourself with unrealistic expectations.

Exercise for Body and Mind

Exercise isn't just about building muscle or improving physical fitness; it's also about boosting **mental and emotional well-being**. Regular exercise has been proven to improve mood, reduce anxiety, and boost self-esteem. As you continue to work out and build strength, you'll notice improvements in your overall emotional state as well.

Movement builds confidence. It empowers you to take control of your body and your life, fostering a sense of pride in your progress and resilience.

Chapter 7
Nutrition and Recovery

Fueling Your Body for Strength

Let's get one thing straight: I'm not a nutrition expert. I don't have all the answers or a strict regimen, but I **do** understand the importance of fueling your body properly. Nutrition plays a key role in how your body performs, recovers, and grows stronger, especially when you're pushing yourself in the gym and in life. While I don't overeat or binge, I know my eating habits aren't always as **balanced** as they could be. Nutrition is more than just about not overeating—it's about finding that perfect balance to help your body function at its best.

I've learned that it's easy to overlook the importance of nutrition in the middle of working hard, lifting weights, or staying active. We can get caught up in the intensity of physical work and forget that what we put into our bodies directly impacts our progress. Your muscles don't grow just because you hit the gym hard; they grow because you're giving them the **fuel** they need to repair and build. That fuel comes from **balanced nutrition**—not just from protein shakes or the latest trendy diet, but from whole, nutritious foods that support overall health.

The key to fueling your body is finding that balance. I've come to realize that it's not about being perfect or following strict meal plans, but about consistently choosing whole, healthy foods in the right amounts. **A balanced diet** includes a variety of food groups: lean proteins, healthy fats, carbohydrates, and plenty of fruits and vegetables. These nutrients are essential to your performance and your recovery. It's about finding what works for your body, and making sure you're eating in a way that helps you feel energized, focused, and strong.

Here are some **easy nutrition tips for beginners**:
- **Eat a variety of whole foods**: Include a mix of proteins (like chicken, fish, tofu, or beans), carbs (such as brown rice, oats, or sweet potatoes), and healthy fats (like avocado, nuts, and olive oil) in your meals.
- **Stay hydrated**: Water is vital for muscle recovery and energy. Make sure you're drinking plenty of water throughout the day.
- **Don't skip meals**: Your body needs consistent fuel to keep your metabolism and energy levels stable. Skipping meals or going too long without eating can leave you feeling sluggish or affect your performance.
- **Listen to your body**: If you're hungry, eat. If you're full, stop. Trust your body's cues and adjust portions as needed.
- **Prioritize protein**: Protein is key for muscle repair and growth. Make sure you're getting enough, especially after workouts.

While I'm not perfect, and my eating habits aren't always as balanced as they could be, I understand that the better I take care of my body through nutrition, the better it will serve me in the gym and in life.

Rest and Recovery

Rest is one of the most **underrated** parts of fitness. We often think that if we're not working hard, we're not making progress. But the truth is, **rest is when the real magic happens**. It's during recovery that your body rebuilds and grows stronger.

I've learned this through experience. It's easy to get caught up in the mindset that the harder you work, the better the results, but that's not the full picture. While pushing yourself is essential, **recovery** is just as important. It's in the moments of rest that your muscles repair and rebuild, allowing you to come back stronger for your next workout.

For me, **recovery isn't just about rest days**, it's also about good sleep, managing stress, and allowing my body to repair. Sleep is a key component of recovery because it's when your muscles actually rebuild. If you're not getting enough sleep, you're robbing yourself of the opportunity to fully recover and grow.

Rest and recovery aren't signs of weakness—they're part of the process. They're the times when you allow your body to heal and rebuild. Without enough rest, you can risk overtraining, injury, and burnout. It's about finding that balance between hard work and allowing yourself to rest. Overtraining leads to fatigue and can actually hinder your progress. **Rest is a vital part of the cycle of growth.**

Here are some tips on **rest and recovery**:

- **Prioritize sleep**: Aim for 7-9 hours of quality sleep per night. This is when your body does most of its healing and rebuilding.
- **Take active rest**: On rest days, you don't have to be completely inactive. Try light activities like walking, stretching, or yoga to keep your body moving without overexerting yourself.
- **Listen to your body**: If you're feeling drained, sore, or fatigued, give yourself permission to take a break. Pushing through exhaustion can lead to injury.
- **Incorporate stretching and mobility exercises**: These can help with muscle recovery, improve flexibility, and reduce the risk of injury.

Remember, it's not about being on a never-ending treadmill of exercise; it's about creating a **cycle of effort and recovery**. Pushing your limits is important, but **taking the time to rest and recover is equally as essential**.

Chapter 8
Overcoming Mental Hurdles

Mindset is Everything

When it comes to your fitness journey, **mindset is the foundation**. It doesn't matter how strong your body gets if your mind isn't in the right place. The way you think about your abilities, challenges, and progress directly impacts your success. Positive thinking isn't just about looking on the bright side — it's about developing the mental resilience to face obstacles head-on and keep moving forward.

It's easy to let negative thoughts creep in, especially when things aren't going as planned. You might catch yourself thinking, "I'm not strong enough," or "I'll never be able to do that." The power of **positive thinking** isn't just in optimism; it's in **rewiring your brain** to focus on solutions, opportunities, and growth, instead of dwelling on limitations.

Shifting negative thoughts takes practice. When a negative thought arises, try to reframe it in a positive light. For example, if you think, "I'll never get stronger," reframe it to, "I'm getting stronger every day, and every effort counts." It's about training yourself to see setbacks as temporary and part of the process. **A growth mindset** is one that sees challenges as opportunities to learn, improve, and push your boundaries.

To build a growth mindset, try the following strategies:
- **Affirmations**: Repeating positive statements about yourself and your abilities can help rewire your brain and replace negative thinking with confidence. For example, say, "I am strong," or "I am capable."

- **Focus on progress, not perfection**: Every step you take, no matter how small, is a victory. Celebrate small milestones and remind yourself how far you've come.
- **Learn from mistakes**: Instead of beating yourself up for failing, ask yourself, "What can I learn from this?" Mistakes are opportunities for growth, not signs of failure.

Dealing with Setbacks and Staying Resilient

Setbacks are inevitable. There will be days when you feel like you're not making progress or when life throws you a curveball. **Resilience** is what helps you stay in the game when things get tough. It's about **bouncing back**, staying motivated, and finding the strength to keep going even when the road seems hard.

Coping strategies for tough days can make a huge difference in how quickly you recover. When things don't go as planned, take a step back and breathe. Here are some tips for dealing with setbacks:

- **Take a break**: It's okay to step away when you're feeling overwhelmed. Give yourself permission to rest without guilt.
- **Revisit your goals**: When you face a setback, revisit why you started. **Remind yourself of your bigger goals** and how important they are to you.
- **Talk to someone**: Sometimes, you just need to express how you feel. Talk to a friend, family member, or a support group. They can help you process emotions and gain a new perspective.
- **Small victories matter**: Focus on what you've accomplished, not what you haven't. Recognize the strength it takes to keep going despite the challenges.

When it comes to bouncing back from failure, remember that **failure isn't final**. Failure is just a part of the process. The most successful people aren't those who never fail — they're the ones who keep getting up every time they fall. It's about **resilience**: the ability to keep moving forward, even when you feel like giving up.

Chapter 9
Empowering Yourself and Others

The Impact of Your Journey

One of the most powerful aspects of your journey is **the impact it can have on others**. Your story — your challenges, your triumphs, your resilience — can inspire others to take action, make changes in their own lives, and pursue their goals, no matter their circumstances. You may not realize it, but by simply sharing your experiences, you become a beacon of hope for others who are walking a similar path.

Your journey can serve as a reminder that **strength comes in many forms**, and no matter where we start, we can all build something powerful. Every time you share your story, you're showing someone else that it's possible to overcome adversity, reclaim strength, and continue growing. **Your journey is a form of empowerment** that extends far beyond your own growth.

The importance of sharing your experiences cannot be overstated. When you lift others up, you not only empower them but also yourself. **Community support is powerful**, and by being open about your struggles and victories, you build a network of people who understand, support, and cheer you on.

Becoming Your Best Self

This journey isn't just about fitness. It's about becoming the best version of yourself, in every area of your life. As you continue to grow physically, don't forget about **the emotional and mental aspects of**

your journey. Cultivate self-love and **confidence** in every step you take.

Building self-confidence is not a one-time thing. It's a continuous process that requires you to recognize your own worth and embrace who you are. **Self-love** is about accepting yourself, flaws and all, and recognizing your strengths and potential. The stronger you become, the more confident you'll feel in your ability to tackle anything that comes your way.

The key to becoming your best self is **progress, not perfection**. There will be ups and downs, but each day brings a new opportunity to learn, grow, and refine your path. Keep investing in yourself, keep believing in your journey, and keep striving to be the person you want to be — inside and out.

Continuing the Journey of Growth, Both In and Outside the Gym

Your journey of growth doesn't end when you leave the gym. In fact, the real test is how you continue to apply the lessons you've learned in your everyday life. The discipline, the resilience, the mindset you cultivate in the gym can serve you well in all aspects of life. Whether it's in relationships, work, or personal challenges, the lessons you've learned on this journey are transferable.

Chapter 10
The Next Step

Embracing Lifelong Growth

Fitness and personal development aren't just short-term goals; they're **lifelong commitments**. The journey doesn't have a clear finish line. Once you achieve one goal, there's always another challenge to take on. The key to lifelong growth is to **embrace the journey**, knowing that every day is an opportunity to get better — physically, mentally, and emotionally.

As you look ahead, **keep setting new goals**. They can be big or small, but the key is to keep moving forward. Maybe your goal is to improve your personal best in the gym or achieve a new level of mental resilience. Whatever it is, don't stop pushing. **The process of growth is endless.**

Setting Long-Term Goals and Staying Motivated

Long-term goals give you direction and purpose. But staying motivated can be challenging, especially when progress feels slow. Here's how you can stay on track:

- **Break down long-term goals into smaller steps**: This makes them more manageable and keeps you focused on the next step.
- **Visualize your success**: Imagine the person you want to become and how you'll feel once you achieve your goals. This will help you stay motivated during tough times.
- **Celebrate your progress**: Even small wins matter. Every step forward is one step closer to your bigger goals.

Looking to the Future

As you continue your fitness journey, remember that the strength you build — both physical and mental — will serve you in every aspect of your life. **Your strength becomes a foundation for the future.** It helps you face challenges with confidence, pursue new opportunities, and inspire others along the way.

The journey never ends. It's a continuous process of **empowerment, self-discovery, and growth**. Your story is far from finished, and as you continue to learn, adapt, and grow, you'll realize that **the best is yet to come. Embrace the future with open arms**, and keep pushing forward, knowing that your strength, perseverance, and mindset will guide you to an even brighter tomorrow.

Chapter 11
Thriving Beyond the Gym

Fitness is often the spark that ignites a larger transformation. It's about more than lifting weights or rolling onto a treadmill; it's about cultivating strength, discipline, and resilience that ripple into every corner of life. In this chapter, we explore how the habits and lessons built in the gym can empower you far beyond its walls.

1. Applying Your Strength to Everyday Life

The strength you've built isn't just physical — it's mental, emotional, and spiritual. These forms of strength show up in ways you may not expect:

- **In Relationships**: Fitness teaches patience, dedication, and communication with yourself. These qualities translate into being a better friend, partner, or family member, able to handle conflicts and connect with empathy.
- **At Work**: The discipline of showing up, even when it's hard, mirrors the persistence needed to tackle professional challenges or chase career goals.
- **In Personal Growth**: Fitness shows you that growth is possible, no matter how daunting the starting line feels. This belief can fuel pursuits like learning a new skill, starting a hobby, or tackling a long-held dream.

2. The Power of Routine in Life

Consistency is the backbone of success in fitness, and it's just as crucial outside the gym. The habits you've formed — whether it's showing up to train or planning your week — are tools you can use in all areas of life.

- **Building Healthy Daily Habits**: Whether it's sticking to a morning routine or carving out time for reflection, consistency helps you create a stable foundation for growth.
- **Time Management**: Just like structuring a workout, learning to prioritize and manage your time effectively can help balance the demands of work, relationships, and personal health.
- **Overcoming Overwhelm**: Breaking life's big tasks into manageable steps, just like you do with fitness goals, makes challenges feel achievable.

3. Building a Community of Support

The people around you have a profound impact on your mindset and motivation. In the gym, you may have found encouragement from trainers, peers, or fellow gym-goers. That same principle applies to life:

- **Surrounding Yourself with Positivity**: Seek out friends, colleagues, and mentors who support your growth and celebrate your victories.
- **Finding Shared Purpose**: Connecting with others who have similar experiences — like fellow wheelchair users or amputees — creates a network of mutual understanding and encouragement.
- **Giving as Well as Receiving**: Just as others lift you up, offer support and motivation in return. It creates a cycle of positivity and progress that benefits everyone.

4. Giving Back and Inspiring Others

Your journey doesn't just belong to you; it has the potential to inspire and uplift those around you. By sharing your story, you can spark motivation and hope in others who may be struggling to take their first steps (or rolls).

- **Mentorship**: Offering guidance or encouragement to someone just starting their journey can be incredibly rewarding.
- **Sharing Your Story**: Whether it's through social media, a community event, or simply a conversation, your experience can resonate with others and show them what's possible.
- **Creating Change**: Advocating for inclusivity, accessibility, and representation in fitness and beyond can make a lasting impact.

5. Continuing to Set New Goals

Fitness teaches us that the journey doesn't end with reaching a single goal. It's a continuous process of striving for new heights, learning, and growing.

- **Embracing New Challenges**: Whether it's mastering a new skill, taking on a fitness milestone, or setting personal or professional goals, growth happens when you step outside your comfort zone.
- **Recognizing the Ripple Effect**: When you set and achieve goals in one area of life, it boosts your confidence and ambition in others.
- **Living with Purpose**: Goals give life direction, and the act of pursuing them brings fulfillment and meaning.

6. Living Your Life to the Fullest

At its core, thriving beyond the gym means living with confidence and authenticity. You've already proven to yourself that you're stronger than your challenges. Now, it's about carrying that strength into everything you do.

- **Celebrate Your Wins**: No matter how small, every victory is a testament to your persistence and growth.
- **Take Pride in Your Journey**: Your story is unique and powerful. Own it, share it, and let it drive you forward.

- **Stay Open to What's Next**: Life is full of opportunities to grow, connect, and thrive. Embrace them wholeheartedly, knowing you have the tools to succeed.

Chapter 12
Your Legacy of Strength

As we come to the final chapter of this journey, I want to leave you with something that transcends the gym, fitness, or even the physical transformation you've undergone. The journey you've embarked on is not just about overcoming the challenges of today — it's about the lasting impact you leave behind. Your strength is a legacy that can inspire others, shape your future, and echo in the lives of those you touch.

1. Reflecting on How Far You've Come

Take a moment and look back. Think of where you started, the obstacles you faced, and the strength it took to get where you are today. Often, we get so caught up in the next goal or the next step that we forget to pause and appreciate the growth we've achieved.

- **Celebrate Your Journey**: Recognize how far you've come, not just in terms of your physical abilities, but in your mindset, resilience, and emotional strength. Every step, every challenge, every setback you overcame is a victory.

- **Personal Transformation**: The person you were before this journey is not the same person you are now. You've shed limitations, doubts, and fears, and embraced new possibilities. Take pride in the courage it took to start, to keep going, and to never give up.

2. Defining Your Legacy

Your journey is a story that matters, not just for you, but for everyone around you. Your legacy isn't about fame or grandeur — it's about the impact you make on others and the example you set.

- **The Ripple Effect**: Every time you push through a difficult workout, every time you share your story, you're creating a ripple effect. Your persistence, your vulnerability, your triumphs — they don't just belong to you; they inspire others.
- **Leaving a Mark**: Whether it's through mentoring someone just starting their journey, sharing your story on social media, or simply being an example of resilience to your friends and family, your legacy is defined by how you uplift others and remind them of their own strength.

3. Strength as a Lifelong Journey

The journey of strength isn't linear. It's not about achieving a singular goal and then stopping. It's about continuing to evolve, to learn, and to grow. The strength you've built is something that will serve you for the rest of your life.

- **Embrace Change**: As you grow, you will face new challenges, both in the gym and in life. But remember that the lessons you've learned — how to push through the tough times, how to trust in your abilities, how to persevere — will always be with you.
- **Lifelong Growth**: Strength doesn't have a finish line. There's always room for improvement, whether it's pushing through a new physical challenge, diving deeper into your personal development, or evolving in your relationships. Growth is a continuous, beautiful process.

4. Passing the Torch

The most powerful part of your journey is the way it can help light the path for others. The strength you've built can be shared and passed on, inspiring others to take their own first steps toward empowerment.

- **Mentoring Others**: As you move forward in your journey, consider becoming a guide for someone else. Whether it's someone new to the gym, a fellow amputee, or anyone going

through a similar struggle, your experience and wisdom can provide the encouragement they need.
- **The Gift of Inspiration**: Your story has the power to spark hope in someone else. Sharing your challenges, your setbacks, and your triumphs allows others to see that strength isn't something we're born with — it's something we cultivate, moment by moment.

5. Living Boldly and Authentically

At the end of the day, your journey is about more than just physical transformation. It's about living authentically, embracing who you truly are, and living with the confidence that you've faced your fears and emerged stronger.
- **Embrace Your Uniqueness**: You've walked a path that's uniquely yours, and that's something to be proud of. The world needs more people like you — people who aren't afraid to show up as they are, to face adversity with courage, and to stand tall in their authenticity.
- **Live Fully**: Don't wait for the "perfect moment" or for everything to align. Live boldly now, with the strength and confidence you've built. Take risks, chase dreams, and remember that your potential is limitless.

6. The Endless Journey of Strength

The final reminder I want to leave you with is that this is just the beginning. Your journey of strength — physically, mentally, emotionally — is an ongoing process. There's always more to learn, more to achieve, and more lives to touch.
- **An Ongoing Process**: There will be highs and lows, moments of doubt and moments of victory. But through it all, remember that strength is a process, not a destination. The journey you've started today will continue to unfold, and each day will bring new opportunities for growth.

- **A New Chapter**: Your strength doesn't end here. It evolves, it transforms, and it propels you forward, day after day. The future is wide open, and you have everything it takes to embrace it.

A Beautiful Send-Off

As you close this book and reflect on the journey you've just read about, know this: **you are not defined by your limitations or your past, but by your strength, your resilience, and your will to move forward.**

This isn't the end; it's just another beginning. The road ahead is yours to shape, and the strength you've built will carry you through whatever comes next. You have faced challenges, overcome fears, and achieved more than you thought possible. But most importantly, you've discovered that **the true measure of strength is not in what you can do, but in who you become along the way.**

Your journey is an inspiration. Your story matters. And the world is waiting to see just how far your strength will take you.

So, with courage in your heart and fire in your soul, keep moving forward. Keep growing. Keep thriving. **And never forget that you have the power to create the life you deserve — a life full of strength, purpose, and endless possibility.**

Your journey doesn't end here. It's only just begun.

www.ingramcontent.com/pod-product-compliance
Lightning Source LLC
Chambersburg PA
CBHW052044070526
44584CB00018B/2609